FACT OR FAKE ?

THE TRUTH ABOUT
SURVIVAL
SKILLS

ANNABEL SAVERY

First published in Great Britain in 2022 by Wayland
Copyright © Hodder and Stoughton Limited, 2022

Produced for Wayland by
White-Thomson Publishing Ltd
www.wtpub.co.uk

Editor: Annabel Savery
Series Designer: Rocket Design (East Anglia) Ltd
Designer: Clare Nicholas

HB ISBN: 978 1 5263 1854 1
PB ISBN: 978 1 5263 1855 8

Wayland
An imprint of
Hachette Children's Group
Part of Hodder & Stoughton
Carmelite House
50 Victoria Embankment
London EC4Y 0DZ

An Hachette UK Company

www.hachettechildrens.co.uk

Printed in China

Many of the survival skills and activities mentioned in this book are dangerous. You should not attempt to copy them. Always seek the help of a trusted and responsible adult for bushcraft and survival skills. Always tell someone where you are going. If you want to know more about survival or bushcraft skills, ask an adult to look into workshops organised by qualified experts.

Picture acknowledgements:
Shutterstock: Astarina 4, Zaytseva Darya 5 (berry), Vector Tradition 5 (berry face), Anna Tarankova 5 (berry limbs), studiostoks 6, greoli 7, Selin Serhii 8, Ron Leishman 9, 18 (woman), 31, 37, 38, 53 (man), 80 (lion), 93t and 95, Sabelskaya 10, Tronin Andre 11, Sibiryanka 12, Ksuxa-muxa 13, Artelka_Lucky 14–15, Sloth Astronaut 16, masdinnu 17 (flame), Alexander_P 17 (sticks), 45 (tardigrade) and 78 (tap and glass), owatta 18 (glass) and 22, Kwaczek 19 (rope), Kryuchka Yaroslav 19 (climber), 578foot 20, grop 23 (figure), ArtMari 23 (dunes), sivVector 24, shekaka 25, In Art 26 (tornado), parose 26-27 (buildings) , DenisKrivoy 28, Ron and Joe 29, nickolai_self_taught 30 (telescope), Alexandriaandco 30 (blanket), Lexi Claus 32, Abdie 33 (water drop), aksol 33 (desert) , xygami 34, Elina Li 35, Top Vector Studio 36, omibomotu 38 (moon and stars) , Gallinago_media 38 (tree), GoodStudio 39, Gazoukoo 40, Cory Thoman 41, Christopher Hall 42, ianlusung 43, Croisy 44–45, LHF Graphics 45 (magnifying glass), MarijaPiliponyte 46, Cattallina 47 an̶...̶ ... Doodle 53 (lightning), xpixel 54 (raft) , desi̶...̶ ...(figure), Anastasiia Sorokina 57 (avalanche)... An inspiration 63, DOLININAN 64 (scorpio... baldezh 66, Zdenek Sasek 67, T_Dub0v 68... Adrian Hillman 72, Luciano Cosmo 73, Fra... Alfonso 77, aksol 78 (cactus), HitToon 79 (s... 81, Evgeny Komzolov 82–83, falisdeka 84,... Katarina S 89 (cactus) and 92, Dmitry Nata... Gun2becontinued 91 (flame).

All design elements from Shutterstock.

Every effort has been made to clear cop...
please apply to the publisher for rectific...

The website addresses (URLs) included...
However, it is possible that contents or a...
No responsibility for any such changes...

All facts and statistics were correct at th...

CAN YOU SEPARATE THE FACTS FROM THE FAKES?

A DEAD CAMEL MAKES A GREAT SLEEPING BAG

WHAT?!

ANIMALS CAN SMELL FEAR

DEFINITELY!

FEND OFF A CROC BY POKING IT IN THE EYE

NO WAY!

YOU CAN CLEAN WATER WITH SUNLIGHT

REALLY?!

Read on to find out the reality behind popular survival myths and life-saving stories. Discover the truth behind it all and then dazzle your fellow adventurers, friends and family with bizarre, hilarious and totally strange survival skill facts!

YOU CAN LAST LONGER WITHOUT FOOD THAN WITHOUT WATER

FACT OR FAKE?

Depending on what you are up to, the body can last up to 3 days without water. But it can go 30 to 40 days without food. However, this basic guide changes quickly if you are doing exercise or are in a hot place.

TELL ME MORE

The body needs roughly 10 cups of water every day, if you are having a normal day. You lose water through sweating, breathing and when you wee. If it is hot or you are exercising, you lose water faster. Without food, the body can use reserves of fat or muscle for energy, depending on your body type.

NO WATER

Many people have a plentiful water supply, but around the world more than a billion people do not have access to clean water.

VERDICT

Fact

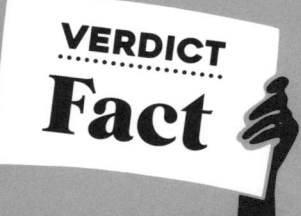

BLACKBERRY PICKING IS THE ONLY THING BRAMBLES —ARE— GOOD FOR

I'm good for more than just pie!

FACT OR FAKE?

Blackberries are the fruit of brambles, which are spiky, twisting plants that grow in hedgerows and on open land. While you may have picked blackberries to eat or use in puddings, there is more to these prickly friends than meets the eye!

TELL ME MORE

For starters, the stems can be eaten, too. You just have to get rid of the prickles first. The leaves can be boiled to make tea. The harder, dryer stems can be used to make fishing lines or string. The leaves can also be used to help soothe burns or swellings. All in all, it's a pretty useful plant if you are stuck in the wilderness.

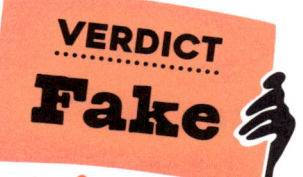

VERDICT
Fake

YOU CAN MAKE STRING FROM NETTLES

FACT OR FAKE?

Imagine you are lost in the woods. You can make a shelter, but you need something to tie it securely and you haven't got any string. Looking around, you spy a stinging nettle ...

TELL ME MORE

Nettles might be irritating when they sting you, but they are very useful. Using gloves, pick a tall nettle carefully, then remove the leaves. The stem is hiding strong, natural string. Once stripped of the stinging hairs, the nettle stem can be crushed and split to take off the tough fibres on the outside. When dry, these can be braided into strong string.

A HELPFUL WEED

String isn't the only use for the helpful nettle – you can cook and eat the leaves, just like spinach, and they can be used medicinally, too. Nettles are also an essential plant for some insects to feed on!

VERDICT

Fact

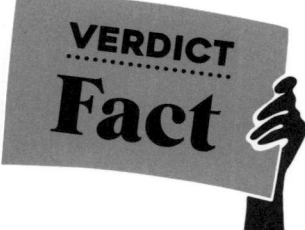

YOU CAN NAVIGATE USING THE STARS ≡ONLY≡ IF YOU ARE AT SEA

FACT OR FAKE?

If you can see the stars in the night sky, then you can use them to navigate by. Finding your way with the stars takes practice, but is a useful skill once you master it. Star navigation is linked with sailors because at sea there are few (if any) other landmarks around. But you can navigate by the stars on dry land, too!

TELL ME MORE

The first step in star gazing is to find key star groups. In the southern hemisphere, you need to look for the Southern Cross. A line between the stars that are furthest apart points south. In the northern hemisphere, look for the Plough. The two outer stars in the Plough's blade line up with the north star, Polaris.

Follow that star!

VERDICT
Fake

FEND OFF A CROC BY POKING IT IN THE EYE

You poked me in the eye!

It's hard to imagine being in a situation where you would need to fight off a crocodile. However, if it does happen, you may be able to get away by going for its eyes. These, along with its throat and nostrils, are the croc's most sensitive parts.

There are over 20 species of crocodilians, a group that includes crocodiles, alligators, caimans and gharials. While some are not big enough to be a danger to humans, others are. The best way to stay safe is to make sure you know which rivers have crocodiles in and keep your distance!

BIG BITE

The Nile crocodile is one of the biggest crocodilians and has a bite that is nearly 5,000 times more powerful than a human's.

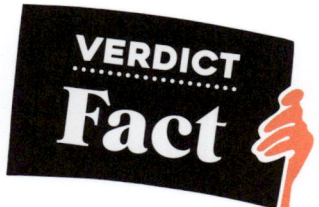

VERDICT
Fact

Never mind shelter, where's my supper?

FOOD IS THE FIRST THING YOU NEED TO LOOK FOR WHEN LOST

FACT OR FAKE?

A rumbling tummy after a long day's walking might make food seem like the most important thing in the world. But if you find yourself lost in the woods, there are a few things that need to be done before you start looking for supper.

TELL ME MORE

Firstly, you need to find a safe place – away from animals and any other dangerous things like falling rocks or cliffs. Then you need to make a shelter. Your body can go for a good amount of time without food (see page 4), but not for long without water. When lost, try to keep safe, warm and hydrated while you work out how to get help.

VERDICT

Fake

9

TREES CAN TELL YOU WHICH WAY TO GO

This way!

The good thing about using trees is that they are around all the time when other navigation tools, such as the Sun and stars, are not. It is best to find an isolated tree and to walk around it a few times at a distance to see its structure.

TELL ME MORE

Trees are not symmetrical, the way they grow is affected by their environment. In the northern hemisphere, the south side of the tree will get the most sunlight and so will grow fullest with more horizontal branches. The side in the tree's own shade is likely to have fewer leaves and upward reaching branches. In the southern hemisphere, the fullest side of the tree will be the north side.

MOSS MYTH

There is a myth that moss grows on the north side of trees (or the south in the southern hemisphere). This tip is likely to be false as moss will grow wherever it likes!

VERDICT
Fact

YOU CAN SUCK THE VENOM OUT OF A SNAKE BITE

FACT OR FAKE?

This is one of those myths that has been made famous by films, but doesn't actually work. The person sucking the wound may take in snake venom and their spit may contain germs that could cause infection.

TELL ME MORE

If someone is bitten by a snake, the best thing to do is to apply pressure and a bandage to the wound and to seek help immediately. It might help for the victim to remove any tight clothing in case the bite causes swelling. It is also important to remember what the snake looks like, so that you can describe it to the emergency services.

VERDICT
Fake

YOU CAN USE YOUR WATCH AS A COMPASS

This works only if you use an analogue watch with hands that tick around in a circle. Sadly, this won't work with a digital or smart watch. Oh, and you will need the Sun, too ...

TELL ME MORE

To convert your watch to a compass in the northern hemisphere, you need to line the hour hand up with the Sun. Then, find the spot halfway between the 12 and the hour hand. This is south. In the southern hemisphere, you need to line the number 12 up with the Sun. The mark halfway between the 12 and the hour hand, marks north.

VERDICT
Fact

EATING SNOW IS AS GOOD AS DRINKING WATER

FACT OR FAKE?

If you run out of drinking water when out in the snow, you might think the snow is the next best thing. It's just frozen water, right? Wrong. Snow is actually mostly air, so you'd need a lot of snow to make up the same amount of water.

TELL ME MORE

Even if you could eat enough snow, you probably still wouldn't stay hydrated. Your body would have to work hard to warm up the cold snow that you take in. This activity would use up more water in your body, causing you to dehydrate further. The best thing to do if out in the snow is to melt some snow before drinking it.

SNOWBALLS

If you are stuck, snow is better than no water at all. You can squash it into a small ball and suck on it, your mouth melting it a little at a time.

VERDICT
Fake

PICKING WILD MUSHROOMS CAN BE
VERY
DANGEROUS

Although some mushrooms and fungi look interesting, you really have to know what you are doing if you are going to pick them. The problem is that poisonous mushrooms can look extremely similar to those that are safe to eat. Even getting their chemicals on your hands can be dangerous.

VERDICT

Fact

14

TELL ME MORE

There are over 10,000 known species of mushroom. Of these, some are just not edible: they are too tough or chewy. Some will make you unwell; some will cause death. Some are edible, but not very tasty, and a few are really delicious. The best advice is to go picking with someone who really knows their deadly from their delicacies!

NASTY NAMES
Many deadly mushrooms have deadly-sounding names: the sickener, poison pie, fool's funnel, deadly webcap, devil's bolete, destroying angel ...

A SHELTER'S JOB IS TO KEEP OUT THE RAIN

FACT OR FAKE?

A shelter is more than a roof over your head. The best shelter to make depends on your surroundings, but you need to remember to protect yourself from more than just rain.

TELL ME MORE

Your shelter must protect you from all weathers, including wind and sun, as well as rain. It is also important to have some layers below you to insulate you from the ground, which will make you cold. If you can make a fire, it needs to be close enough to give you warmth, but not close enough to set the shelter on fire!

WEARING WONDERS

If you're making a shelter it may help to look at your clothes. Shoelaces and torn fabric strips are super helpful for securing branches.

VERDICT

....

Fake

16

YOU CAN START A FIRE WITH STICKS

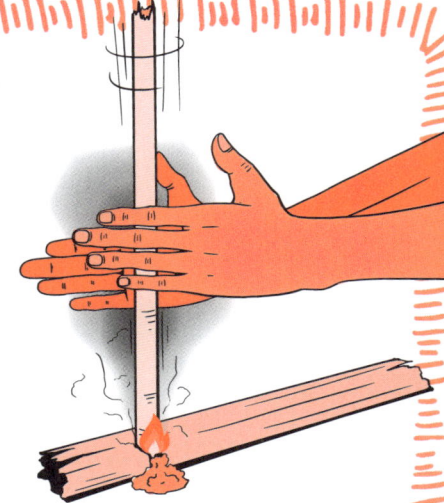

FACT OR FAKE?

You can! But it is pretty hard work. Most importantly you will need dry sticks, then you will need a lot of patience. Before starting, you will need to collect tinder, which is dry material such as seed heads, and small kindling sticks to keep the fire going once started.

TELL ME MORE

To make a fire with sticks you use friction. The action of rubbing two things against each other makes heat. Eventually, you may be able to make a tiny glowing ember. If you do get an ember, you need to add the tinder and blow very gently. Hopefully, the fire will catch and you then need to keep it going!

SPLASH!

Starting a fire this way is hard work and can make you sweat. Beware of a drop of sweat extinguishing your hard-earned glowing ember!

VERDICT
Fact

17

YOU CAN DRINK YOUR OWN WEE TO SURVIVE

FACT OR FAKE?

In an extreme situation, with no water and no hope of finding any, you might think wee is the best thing to drink. In certain situations, it might be better than nothing. But drinking urine can also cause more problems than it solves.

TELL ME MORE

Although urine contains around 95 per cent water, it also contains salt and urea. Urea is made up of the waste products your body doesn't need and is filtered out of your system by your kidneys. Drinking salty urine causes you to dehydrate further and makes your kidneys work harder to filter out more urea.

SPACE WATER

Water is such a precious thing on the International Space Station that astronauts have to save every drop. All waste water, including wee, is put through a filtration system so that the astronauts can drink it again!

VERDICT
Fake

YOU MUST NEVER CUT A CLIMBING ROPE

FACT OR FAKE?

In ordinary circumstances, no, you should never cut a climbing rope. But an extraordinary situation might call for extraordinary actions. Joe Simpson and Simon Yates were climbing in the Peruvian Andes when disaster struck: Joe slipped and broke his leg.

TELL ME MORE

Simon managed to lower Joe down some of the mountain on a rope, but then, in the dark, Joe went over a cliff edge. Simon was pulled towards the edge as Joe fell. After some time, Simon made the difficult decision to cut the rope rather than being pulled over the edge by Joe's weight. Joe landed in a crevasse and, amazingly, he managed to crawl to safety. They both survived, and with no hard feelings.

VERDICT

PART **Fake**

PART **Fact**

SHOUT LOUDLY IF YOU GET LOST

FACT OR FAKE?

Although shouting for help might seem obvious when you are lost, unless you know there is someone nearby, it may not be the best idea. Calling for help will use up vital energy reserves that you will need if you are going to make a shelter and keep safe in the wild.

TELL ME MORE

While shouting your head off may not be a good idea, making noise certainly is. A whistle is a great bit of kit to keep in your bag in case you need help. If you don't have a whistle, banging sticks or anything metal together will help people to find you and may also keep wild animals away.

PEEP PEEP PEEP

S.O.S. is a universal distress signal (see page 29) Three short, three long and three short blows on a whistle will let people know that you need help.

VERDICT
Fake

YOU SHOULD KEEP YOUR ADVENTURE LOCATIONS A SECRET

FACT OR FAKE?

In April 2003, Aron Ralston went to explore Bluejohn Canyon in Utah, USA. It's a 17-km-long crack in the earth, at some places only a metre wide. He hadn't told anyone where he was climbing and his adventure became a nightmare.

TELL ME MORE

Aron had climbed on his own many times, but on this day an accident happened. Aron's arm was trapped by a falling boulder. To get out of the canyon, Aron had to cut the lower part of his arm off. Incredibly, he survived and was able to get to help. One of the most important rules of hiking, climbing and other outdoor sports is to always tell someone where you are going and when you expect to be back.

FILM TIME
Aron's story was made into a film called *127 Hours*, in 2010.

VERDICT
....
Fake

21

S.T.O.P.
IF YOU GET LOST

FACT OR FAKE?

This is a great acronym to remember if you are out and about. S.T.O.P. stands for Stop Think Observe Plan, and these four letters might just save your life!

TELL ME MORE

The first thing to remember when you realise you are lost is the **S** – STOP. It may be your instinct to rush to try and find a way back to the path, but it is better to stop and wait for your feelings of panic to settle down. Then you can **T**hink clearly what to do next, **O**bserve anything around you that may help, and **P**lan your next move.

VERDICT
Fact

22

I'm lost!

YOU COULD SURVIVE GETTING LOST IN THE SAHARA DESERT

SO BIG!

The size of the Sahara Desert is around 9.2 million square km. It is the world's biggest dry desert. Getting lost here is a BAD idea!

FACT OR FAKE?

It's a big ask, but Mauro Prosperi has done it! He began an ultra-marathon, got lost in a sandstorm and managed to walk over 300 km to safety.

TELL ME MORE

When Prosperi was caught in the sandstorm, he was separated from his fellow runners. Many search parties looked for him, with no luck. He says he ate birds' eggs, bats and beetles to survive. He walked only at early morning and early evening, found shade during the day, and kept warm at night by sleeping under the sand.

VERDICT
Fact*

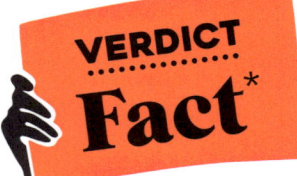

*But we don't recommend getting lost in any desert.

PREPPERS
ARE PEOPLE GETTING READY FOR ADVENTURE

Actually, preppers are people getting ready for survival. They are sometimes also known as survivalists. They gather equipment and learn skills that would enable them to survive without 'normal society' in the event of a world disaster.

TELL ME MORE

Prepping comes from the word preparing. Prepping can include getting supplies of long-life food ready, learning first aid and self-defence skills, and practising wild camping and foraging skills. Some people prepare by building bunkers: secure or underground living spaces that they could survive inside for a limited time.

VERDICT
Fake

BUG OUT
'Bug out' is a military term that means to leave everything quickly. It is used by preppers, too!

24

ANTARCTIC EXPLORERS ATE THEIR DOGS

Ate their whaaat?!

FACT OR FAKE?

Desperate times call for desperate measures. Explorers Mawson, Ninnis and Mertz set out from their Antarctic base camp in 1912 to explore the land eastwards. They had provisions and equipment for two months on sledges pulled by dogs.

TELL ME MORE

The team of three were part of Douglas Mawson's Australian Antarctic Expedition. They met tragedy when Ninnis fell into a crevasse with most of the provisions, equipment and dogs. Mertz and Mawson went on, eventually having to eat the remaining dogs to survive. Mertz later died, but Mawson went on alone for 30 more days. When he finally reached base camp, the pickup boat had just left!

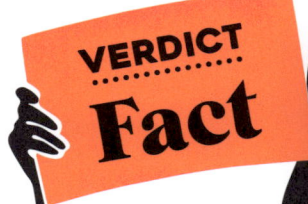

VERDICT
Fact

DARK AND LIGHT
In the Antarctic summer it is light all the time. The winter then brings 6 months of darkness.

YOU COULD SURVIVE BEING CARRIED BY A TORNADO

VERDICT Fact

FACT OR FAKE?

When a tornado struck Missouri, USA, in 2006, it sucked the windows and doors off Matt Suter's mobile home. It then sucked him out too, throwing him 398 m into a field. He was knocked unconscious, but was otherwise unharmed.

TELL ME MORE

In the US, there can be over 1,000 tornadoes each year, and many deaths. However, Suter isn't the first to survive a tornado flight: cows, pigs and dogs have all been recorded taking tornado flights. In 1999 in Oklahoma, USA, a baby survived a 30 m tornado flight, and in 1955 in South Dakota, USA, a girl and her pony were whizzed 300 m and lived to tell the tale.

MEASURING TORNADOES

The scale used to classify tornado strength is called the Enhanced Fujita (EF) scale. Grades are from EF0 to EF5. The Missouri tornado was an EF2 with wind speeds of up to 252 kph!

REMEMBER NOSE AND TOES IF YOU FALL IN THE RAPIDS

FACT OR FAKE?

Going on a rafting adventure is exciting, but you should always listen to the safety advice given. This might include the phrase 'nose and toes', which is going to be really important if you end up in the rapids!

TELL ME MORE

If you do fall off a raft, your boatmates should be able to pull you back on or to throw you a rope. But in a fast-moving river, you can get swept away from the raft. If this happens, try not to panic. Turn on to your back and lift your legs up. Your nose and toes need to be out of the water. Use your arms to turn your body to face downstream, with your toes in front of you, and keep your arms out wide to help to slow you down.

PULL!

If you do get thrown a rope, stay on your back while they pull you in, so your mouth doesn't get filled with water!

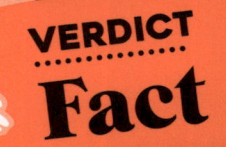

VERDICT

Fact

S.O.S.
MEANS SAVE OUR SOULS

> SAVE OUR SOULS

FACT OR FAKE?

In 1906 an international committee decided that S.O.S. should be used as an international distress signal. But rather than meaning Save Our Souls or Save Our Ship, the letters don't mean anything at all!

TELL ME MORE

The letters weren't even the reason for the signal being chosen. Rather, it was decided that ········· from the Morse code system would be easy to recognise and hard to mistake for anything else. It could also be understood in any language, which removed the problem of different countries having their own distress signals, as this had caused a lot of confusion.

HELP!

As technology advanced and written and voice messages could be sent, 'MAYDAY' replaced S.O.S. as a signal of distress.

VERDICT

Fake

EMERGENCY BLANKETS ARE USED ON SPACE TELESCOPES

I'm so warm and cosy

FACT OR FAKE?

Invented by NASA (National Aeronautics and Space Administration) in 1964, thin, silver emergency blankets have become a familiar part of any survival kit. They are used to maintain temperatures on space tech and can maintain body heat, too!

TELL ME MORE

The material NASA invented is a type of plastic coated with aluminium. It was developed to be lightweight, so that it didn't add to the weight of space equipment. It had to insulate equipment in space, where temperatures can vary wildly. Originally made to protect rockets and rovers, it now also protects marathon runners, explorers, satellites and more!

IT'S EVERYWHERE

Space blanket material has been used on countless projects: from the Apollo lunar landing vehicles to the James Webb Space Telescope!

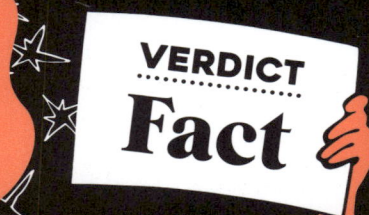

VERDICT

Fact

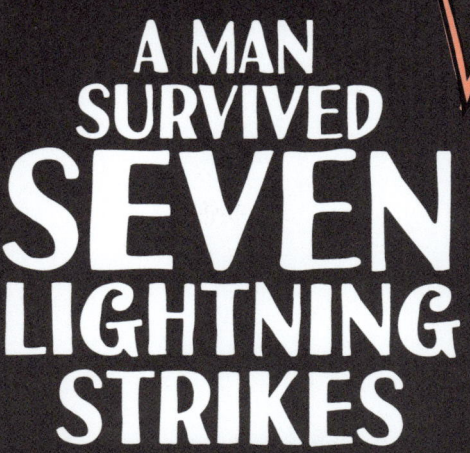

A MAN SURVIVED SEVEN LIGHTNING STRIKES

Not again!

FACT OR FAKE?

Roy Sullivan grew up in the Blue Ridge mountains, USA. In 1936, he became a Shenandoah National Park ranger. Although the saying goes, 'lightning never strikes twice in the same place', Sullivan reported being struck seven times between 1942 and 1977.

TELL ME MORE

The first strike in 1942 happened when Sullivan was running from a burning fire tower that had been struck. The second struck through the window of a truck he was driving. Each strike left him with minor injuries, but he survived.

VERDICT
Fact

HOW LIKELY?

In 2019, the US National Weather Service put the odds of getting struck by lightning that year at 1 in 1,222,000!

Nom, nom

IF YOU SEE AN ANIMAL EATING FOOD, THAT FOOD IS SAFE FOR HUMANS, TOO

FACT OR FAKE?

You might think that most mammals are alike, that if a squirrel eats something, you can too. Or how about a bird? If a bird munches on some bright berries, surely they are safe for you to eat? Wrong. Animals, particularly birds, can eat lots of things that are dangerous to humans.

TELL ME MORE

Birds can eat berries that are poisonous for humans because birds have different chemicals in their digestive systems. Berries are an essential part of many birds' winter diet, especially when the ground is too hard for them to find grubs and insects. Squirrels and other small mammals can eat some nuts and mushrooms that could poison us.

VERDICT
Fake

VERY BERRY
Surviving is exactly what berries do best. They feed birds, and in return, birds spread seeds and more berry plants grow!

YOU CAN MAKE WATER IN THE DESERT

Sure I can make water ...

Desert Water Recipe Book

FACT OR FAKE?

Out in the desert, the chances of stumbling upon a natural water source are slim. The solar still is a clever way of collecting water when there appears to be none. It uses the greenhouse effect.

TELL ME MORE

First you dig a hole and place a container in the centre. Then you cover the hole with a clear plastic sheet and weigh the sheet down around the edges. Next, place a small rock in the centre of the sheet directly above your water container. The Sun's heat passes through the plastic. Water in the ground evaporates, then condenses on the underside of the plastic. The water droplets run to the centre and drip into your container.

VERDICT
Fact

A HOT TUB IS THE BEST WAY TO WARM UP

Mmm toasty!

FACT OR FAKE?

While it might sound great to jump into a tub of really hot water when you are freezing cold, it could actually be very dangerous and painful. The sudden temperature change can cause your body to go into shock and could even cause a heart attack.

TELL ME MORE

The best way to warm up is by warming the middle areas of your body first, for example by placing warm water bottles under your armpits. Snuggling up to someone who is warm is another good option. You should also remove any wet clothing and wrap up in something warm and dry.

TOO COLD!
The body's usual temperature is around 37°C. When the body temperature drops below 35°C it starts to struggle and this is called hypothermia.

VERDICT
....
Fake

BOILING WATER MAKES IT SAFE TO DRINK

Natural water sources may look crystal clear and clean, but they are actually home to many pathogens, parasites and bacteria – all of which can make you ill. As it can be hard to tell how clean water is, it's safest to boil it up before drinking it.

TELL ME MORE

Boiling up water will kill any invisible and harmful microorganisms hiding in it. When setting out on an adventure where you cannot carry enough water with you, always make sure you have the equipment to boil water.

VERDICT
Fact

WONDER WORMS

Tapeworms lay eggs in water. If drunk, the tapeworm eggs hatch and can live inside the human gut for up to 30 years, growing up to 24 m long!

YOU CAN SEND AN S.O.S USING SMOKE

FACT OR FAKE?

If you've built up a fire and you think rescue services may be looking for you, you might help them out by sending a signal. Once your fire is strong enough, add on green leafy branches for white smoke or rubber and plastic for black smoke.

TELL ME MORE

As well as changing the colour of smoke that a fire makes, you can use a blanket to send an S.O.S. signal (see page 29). Wafting the blanket in the smoke will create shapes to represent the dots and dashes. Be careful not to get the blanket to close to the fire though!

VERDICT
Fact

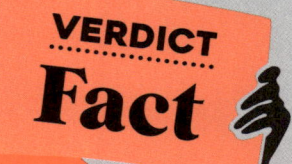

TREEHUGGING CAN SAVE YOUR LIFE

Now I'm safe

According to one survival expert based in northern Sweden – if you hug a tree, you'll stay in one place and you won't feel so alone. Staying put is important if you are lost. Wandering about will make it harder for a search party to find you and will tire you out.

TELL ME MORE

In the wild, weather conditions can worsen quickly and anchoring yourself to something as solid as a tree can give you shelter and stop you feeling so disorientated. At any age, being lost can be frightening. Hugging a tree gives a feeling of safety and keeps you in one place so that help can find you.

HUG TO SURVIVE

Hug-a-Tree and Survive is also the name of a survival initiative set up in North America in the 1980s to teach children about safety in wild places. Today it is run by the National Association for Search and Rescue (NASAR).

VERDICT
Fact

37

IT'S BEST TO WALK IN THE DAY AND SLEEP AT NIGHT

FACT OR FAKE?

Usually this would be true, but how about if you are walking in a desert area? Scorching daytime temperatures and freezing nights might cause you to think again ...

TELL ME MORE

In hot temperatures, your body loses water quickly through sweating and breathing. Walking in cooler temperatures puts less strain on your body. The Grand Canyon National Park, USA, is popular for hiking, but the temperature during the day can rise to over 38°C, while at night it can drop below freezing. So maybe find a shady spot to rest in during the day and hike at cooler times.

START LOOKING

Search and rescue teams are kept busy in Grand Canyon National Park. In 2020 they responded to 235 incidents.

VERDICT

Fake

RELAXED PEOPLE ARE LESS LIKELY TO DROWN

FACT OR FAKE?

If you fall suddenly into water, it will be hard not to feel a sense of panic. However, the more relaxed you are, the more likely you are to survive.

TELL ME MORE

If you can relax in the water, you are more likely to be able to float. Your body is naturally buoyant – which means it will normally rise to the surface. Floating on your back is easiest as it will also keep your face above water, allowing you to breathe. If you float on your front, keep raising your head above the water to take a fresh breath of air.

VERDICT

Fact

SHIVERING IS NOTHING TO WORRY ABOUT

The most important thing when you are out in the cold is to stay alert and to pay attention to what your body is up to. If you start shivering, it might not be a big deal, you can soon warm yourself up. But if you are still shivering 10 to 15 minutes later, your warm-up isn't working well enough.

TELL ME MORE

Once you've been shivering for 10 minutes or longer, you need to take it as a warning sign and do something more effective to warm yourself up. Shivering is caused by the body trying to make heat. Using energy like this will make you feel tired, and it will become harder to perform important tasks and get help.

I'm fine

MUSCLE MOVES

Shivering is an involuntary muscle movement — you can't control it. Your body will stop on its own when it is warm enough.

VERDICT
Fake

40

QUICKSAND
WILL SWALLOW YOU UP
IN MINUTES

FACT OR FAKE?

A bottomless pit of quicksand is the type you see only in films. Most quicksand pools are usually around a metre deep, but they can still be very dangerous and you need to know how to get out of them the right way.

TELL ME MORE

Don't struggle, you are likely to sink deeper. Try to grab hold of something, such as a branch or tree root. Otherwise, lie on your back and try to encourage your legs to float to the surface. Work slowly so you don't get exhausted.

I've got that sinking feeling.

VERDICT
Fake

SPECIAL SAND?
Quicksand isn't a special kind of sand, it's just ordinary sand that has mixed with water coming up from below ground so that it behaves more like a liquid.

41

YOU LOSE MOST HEAT FROM YOUR HEAD

It's true that you should wear a hat if it is really cold, but for the same reason that you wear all your other clothes: shoes, socks, trousers, coat, jumper and so on.

TELL ME MORE

Your body is designed to lose and conserve heat. Your blood is warm and it carries warmth around your body. Where blood vessels travel close to the skin, they lose heat. You have blood vessels under the skin on your head and in cold weather, these will lose heat. But they don't lose heat any faster than any other part of your body.

BRRR!

If you went out in the cold wearing nothing, you would lose about 10 per cent of your body heat through your head!

VERDICT

Fake

YOU COULD LIVE ON TURTLES —AND— RAINWATER

You've got to catch me first!

In 1971, the Robertson family set out from England in a wooden sailing boat, intending to go around the world. They sailed across the Atlantic, visited Caribbean Islands and picked up a hitchhiker. But when they tried to cross the Pacific, their ship was attacked by orcas.

TELL ME MORE

After the boat was wrecked, the family had to make do with a small dinghy and an inflatable raft. After a time, the raft became unusable and their food supplies had gone. They managed to catch turtles, ate the meat and drank the oil and blood. They collected rainwater in containers. After 38 days, the family were picked up by a Japanese fishing trawler.

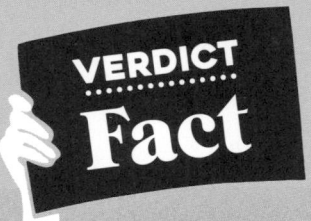

VERDICT
Fact

TOXIC TURTLE
The Robertson family were lucky in their choice of turtle, hawksbill turtle meat can be extremely toxic to humans!

NO LIVING THINGS CAN SURVIVE IN SPACE

FACT OR FAKE?

It's hard to imagine anything living in space: temperatures go from extreme hot to extreme cold. There is no air and the Sun gives out powerful radiation. It takes incredible technology to get a spacecraft to function in space, let alone a living creature.

TELL ME MORE

However, in 2008 a team of scientists launched some brave creatures into space: tardigrades. These microscopic creatures live on Earth, usually in damp mossy places. In space they were exposed to freezing temperatures, radiation, lack of air, dehydration – and some survived!

YOU HAD TO SING TO GO WITH SHACKLETON

FACT OR FAKE?

Around 5,000 people applied to join the explorer Ernest Shackleton on his Antarctic expedition in 1914 – of these, only 26 were chosen. During the interview process they were asked if they could sing!

TELL ME MORE

Shackleton was a great polar explorer. He went twice to the Antarctic before setting out in his ship, *Endurance*, to cross the continent. The ship became stranded in pack ice, was crushed and sank. The crew survived on ice floes until they were able to take small boats to Elephant Island. Shackleton and six men then sailed back to South Georgia to get help, and eventually managed to rescue the rest of the crew.

SURVIVORS

Despite the perils of their failed expedition, not a single member of Shackleton's crew died.

VERDICT
Fact

YOU CAN TELL IF A SNAKE IS VENOMOUS BY THE SHAPE OF ITS EYES

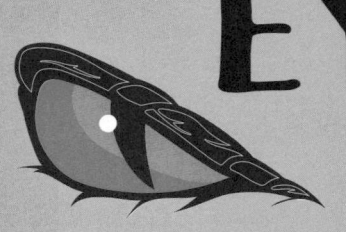

FACT OR FAKE?

If a snake has round pupils in the centre of its eyes, it's harmless. If it has oval or vertical slit-shaped pupils, it is venomous. Actually, this is a myth!

TELL ME MORE

There are lots of so-called tips to identify snakes that are venomous, such as looking at the eyes, the shape of the head, the nose or scales and whether it has a heat-sensing pit or not. What you may be able to tell from the shape of its eyes is whether a snake is active in the day (round pupils) or at night (slit pupils).

POISONOUS OR VENOMOUS?

There are no poisonous snakes! Poisonous things are dangerous if ingested (eaten or drunk); animals that carry venom to inject are called 'venomous'.

VERDICT
....
Fake

47

I think something's about to happen ...

YOUR DOG WILL WARN YOU IF THERE IS GOING TO BE AN EARTHQUAKE

FACT OR FAKE?

For hundreds of years, people have noticed that dogs – and other animals – behave differently before an earthquake. Some people believe that dogs can feel the early tremors that come before an earthquake, which are too small for humans to notice.

TELL ME MORE

However, there is little scientific evidence to say that dogs can sense anything at all until the very last moment before an earthquake. One study in Canada noted that 49 per cent of dogs showed more anxious behaviour before one earthquake, but it is not a broad enough study to be certain.

SNAKE QUAKE

Historians recorded animals, including rats and snakes, deserting a Greek city just days before an earthquake struck in 373 BCE.

VERDICT
(probably)
Fake

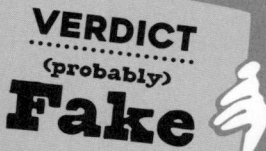

WOMEN CAN SURVIVE LONGER THAN MEN

FACT OR FAKE?

In a starvation situation, it is possible that some women will survive longer than men. Researchers think this is because women can have a naturally higher ratio of body fat to muscle than men. Also, when food becomes scarce, women will burn body fat ahead of muscle tissue.

TELL ME MORE

When desperate for energy, the body will draw on several processes. First it will start to use blood sugar, then it will look for sugar stored in the liver and then it will start using body fat. When the body has used up all fat reserves, it will start to break down muscle tissue, the results of which can be fatal.

DRY DIET

In 1944, two scientists tried to experiment with eating only dry food and drinking no water. One lasted 3 days and the other lasted 4 days before stopping the experiment.

VERDICT
Fact

A DEAD
A GREAT

It happens in films and survival shows, but is it really possible to use a dead animal as a sleeping bag? Survival experts say yes, but it depends on the conditions outside. If it is freezing cold, a large dead animal will give you protection for some time, before the cold freezes it, too!

TELL ME MORE

While an animal carcass may provide shelter from extreme weather conditions, such as a sandstorm or blizzard, it's a worst-case scenario option. There's another problem with a dead-animal sleeping bag: it will attract predators and carrion-feeders looking for their next meal.

HIDE AND SEEK

Films have featured actors hiding inside dead cows, horses and even a crocodile!

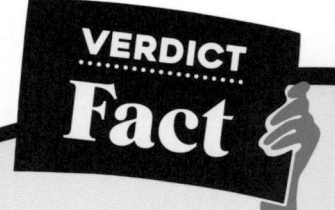

VERDICT
Fact

50

CAMEL MAKES SLEEPING BAG

Hmmmph

YOU SHOULD PRACTISE YOUR SURVIVAL TECHNIQUES

I'm outta here!

FACT OR FAKE?

Many people know about the body's fight-or-flight responses to attack. However, when faced with a disaster, people often respond by freezing – exactly like an animal faced with a predator. Practising survival techniques helps to overcome the first-freeze!

TELL ME MORE

When investigating disasters, researchers also found that many people acted in strange ways, such as worrying about collecting belongings or tidying up. This is because it is hard to think quickly and clearly in an emergency, so we end up doing automatic everyday things. Practising survival techniques, such as fire and earthquake drills, helps them to become more like instant automatic actions if there is an emergency situation.

VERDICT
Fact

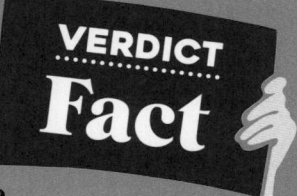

PHOTO TIME
Many people struggle to accept instant danger, even stopping to take photographs of fires or tsunamis!

YOU GET STRUCK BY LIGHTNING ONLY IF YOU ARE HOLDING METAL

FACT OR FAKE?

The age-old advice is not to be holding anything metal when there is a thunderstorm. Tales are told of umbrellas attracting lightning strikes. In reality, a thunderstorm and the lightning it creates are just too big to be affected by a small metal object.

TELL ME MORE

The best place to be during a thunderstorm is inside. If lightning strikes outside, you are unprotected. Buildings can be struck by lightning, but they will conduct the electricity into the ground, not towards you. If you are caught outside, head for an open space away from tall objects, such as trees.

WEARING METAL

Although lightning won't be more attracted to you if you are wearing metal, if by chance you are struck, anything metal on you will become super-hot and could cause burns.

VERDICT

Fake

THE LONGEST TIME LOST AT SEA IS 133 DAYS

FACT OR FAKE?

This record is held by Chinese sailor Poon Lim, but he never intended to set it! He survived a shipwreck, despite being a poor swimmer. Although he saw many vessels, none stopped to pick him up because it was wartime!

TELL ME MORE

Poon Lim was working on a British trading ship. The ship was sunk by a German submarine in 1942. He managed to find one of the ship's rafts in the wreckage, and luckily it had food and water on board! When the supplies ran out, he caught fish and even a small shark. Finally, he was rescued by Brazilian fishermen after 133 days.

SUPPLY TIME

Poon Lim's raft supplies included water, a bag of sugar lumps, beef jerky, lime juice and chocolate!

VERDICT
Fact

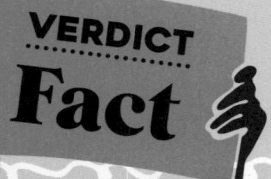

I'll just try again ...

SOME PEOPLE NEVER GIVE UP

FACT OR FAKE?

Norwegian Jan Baalsrud was trained as a spy by the British in the 1940s. In 1943 he accepted a mission to sneak into Nazi-occupied Norway to destroy German equipment and recruit more Norwegian resistance fighters. A mission that went badly wrong!

TELL ME MORE

The Germans were tipped off and destroyed the boat the Norwegians were in. Only Jan made it to shore. His best chance of safety was getting to neutral Sweden. He managed to find local help, but then lost everything in an avalanche. Although he made it to shelter, he then had to amputate his own toes because of frostbite! He was rescued and made it to safety, only to return to the resistance effort once he had recovered.

VERDICT
Fact

YOU ARE SAFE IN THE EYE OF A STORM

FACT OR FAKE?

Although people have spoken of warm weather and blue skies in the eye of a tropical storm, it is still a very dangerous place. Tropical storms keep moving and anyone outside may be caught by the fierce winds of the eye wall.

TELL ME MORE

A hurricane, or tropical storm, brings fierce wind and rain, battering everything in its path. The winds rotate in a circle gradually forming around a central eye. The eyewall surrounds the eye and it is here that the winds are strongest. Near water, waves also tend to rise up inside the eye, making it even more dangerous. Although calm, the area inside the eye will be littered with debris from the storm's path.

STORM NAMES

Tropical storms are given names as they are easier to recognise in a news report than numbers or letters. The names are taken from an alphabetical list. If the hurricane is a really bad one, that name is never used again.

VERDICT

Fake

56

ROLL INTO A **BALL** IF YOU ARE CAUGHT IN AN **AVALANCHE**

FACT OR FAKE?

You hear a rumbling noise, you feel the wind, you look up to see a tumbling wall of snow coming towards you. What do you do?

TELL ME MORE

The first option is to try to get out of the way; run or ski diagonally across the path of the avalanche. Towards the edge of the avalanche the snow's movement will be slower and there is less chance of injury. If you are caught in the middle, you can try to point your feet downhill, so that they take any bumps rather than your head. The other option is to curl in a ball, protecting your head from injury with your arms.

RUSHING RIVER

Avalanches are like fast-flowing rivers of snow. They can reach speeds of 320 kph and gather more snow as they rush along!

VERDICT
Fact

57

A FLOOD HAS TO BE DEEP TO BE DANGEROUS

FACT OR FAKE?

Even though you might think that a small amount of water isn't dangerous, it certainly can be. A parked car could move in just 30 cm of water. You may be knocked over in fast-flowing water, even if it is under knee height.

TELL ME MORE

While you might paddle in the sea or a river up to your waist, flood water is different. It can be fast-flowing and can carry along anything caught in its path – from shopping trolleys to animals. Floating debris can injure you, causing you to fall. Flood water can also be dirty, especially if local water services have been damaged.

MORE FLOODS

Climate change is causing more extreme weather, which has led to more flooding around the world.

VERDICT

Fake

YOU CAN BREATHE THROUGH A REED IF HIDING UNDERWATER

FACT OR FAKE?

You might think this is sure to work, after all, a snorkel works and it's almost the same thing! Well, a snorkel works only because it is short and wide. If you wanted to hide beneath the water, you would need a much longer tube or reed, which then wouldn't work.

TELL ME MORE

Once you are far enough underwater to be hidden, the pressure of the water on your lungs makes it very hard to breathe in. Also, unless you are able to breathe out really hard, you won't force the air to the top of the reed. This means the air you next breathe in will be the same air you just breathed out – which won't do you any good at all!

FAKE FILMS

This trick is used in lots of films and books. It seems like a great way for the good guy to hide from the baddies, but in reality, it won't work!

VERDICT

Fake

VOLCANOES ARE ONLY DANGEROUS IF LAVA FLOWS

FACT OR FAKE?

When you imagine a volcanic eruption, you might think of a slowly sliding river of glowing molten rock. While this is one of the dangers, it's not the only one. When a volcano erupts, clouds of volcanic ash, gas and rock are thrown into the air.

TELL ME MORE

Clouds of hot ash and gas not only cloud the sky, they also make it difficult to breathe. The ash covers just about everything, possibly causing burn injuries and stopping cars and other machines from working. Along with this, when ash and rock land on a glacier it can create a dangerous flow of debris. Rapidly melting ice can also cause deadly mudslides called lahars.

BOOM!
There are around 1,500 active volcanoes around the world, as many as 50 of these can erupt each year!

VERDICT
Fake

YOU SHOULD GET TO HIGH GROUND IF YOU HEAR A TSUNAMI SIREN

FACT OR FAKE?

When an earthquake happens under the ocean, the movement of Earth's tectonic plates creates a tsunami: an enormous wave that rushes across the ocean. As a tsunami approaches the shore, the sea may be pulled outwards. Following this, a series of enormous waves will hit the shore.

TELL ME MORE

It's important to stay alert if you are in a tsunami region and look out for local advice. If you are near the shore, work out how to get to high ground if you need to. If you cannot get clear, you can hold on to something stationary or that will float.

VERDICT
....
Fact

FAST WAVE
A tsunami wave can travel across the ocean at speeds of 800 kph!

BEWARE OF A YAWNING HIPPO

FACT OR FAKE?

Look out for a hippo opening its mouth wide: it might look as if it's having a long, sleepy yawn, but it's actually a sign of aggression. Hippos are big animals, but they are easily startled and are keen to protect their young and their territory.

TELL ME MORE

While they seem calm, hippos can be fierce. If you are in an area with hippos, it is best to keep making noise – if you creep around you might startle a hippo and it will be more likely to attack. Try not to get between the hippo and the water. If you are in a boat, stick to deeper water as hippos often stay in the shallows.

I'm so sleepy

VERDICT
Fact

RUN HIPPO RUN
On land, hippos can reach speeds of 30 kph!

BIRDS ALWAYS FLY TOWARDS WATER

FACT OR FAKE?

If you are in an area you don't know, it may be hard to see where to find water. Watching a flock of birds flying overhead might give you a good clue ... or it might lead you in the wrong direction completely!

TELL ME MORE

While some birds fly towards water, they also fly away again. Depending on the time of day, birds may be heading to water to feed or they may be heading to a safe inland nesting place for the night. While the birds could be one clue, you should try to look for other clues, such as the land sloping downhill, to be more certain of finding water.

FIND THE TRACKS

Land animals may gather at water sources towards the end of the day or evening – look for animal tracks and behaviour to work out which way to go!

VERDICT

Fake

YOU CAN EAT BUGS TO SURVIVE

FACT OR FAKE?

In many parts of the world, eating bugs is completely ordinary. If you are hoping to survive in the wild, eating bugs may be an important part of your diet, but you need to know exactly which ones are safe to eat!

TELL ME MORE

If you can catch them, grasshoppers and crickets are full of protein, but you need to cook them before eating. Ants and termites can be yummy if you can catch enough of them. You could try lifting a log to find some grubs (the young larvae stage of beetles) or try a scorpion for lunch – just be sure to remove the stinger first!

VERDICT
Fact

Erm... are you sure?

BUG BURGERS
Future food shortages could be solved by bugs becoming a larger part of our diets.

YOU CAN SURVIVE IN STYLE

FACT OR FAKE?

While some people prepare for disaster by brushing up on their bushcraft skills and stocking up on tinned food, other people invest in some seriously fancy emergency bunkers!

TELL ME MORE

A basic survival bunker might be a reinforced structure built underground with an emergency power generator and some food. One survival condo in Kansas, USA, however, has many flats with luxury bedrooms, en-suite bathrooms, a gym and pool, washing machines and dryers. It is built inside an old nuclear missile silo!

VERDICT

Fact

(if you are very wealthy!)

SWEET SURVIVAL
In one luxury condo, 75 people could survive underground for five years!

STAND ~IN A~ DOORWAY IF THERE ~IS AN~ EARTHQUAKE

FACT OR FAKE?

A newspaper once printed a picture of a single house doorway still standing after an earthquake. This may have been one of the sources of the myth that a doorway is the best place to stand in an earthquake.

TELL ME MORE

In older houses, the doorway may be a strong part of the house. In modern houses, a doorway is unlikely to be any stronger than any other part of the house. Advice for staying safe in an earthquake is DROP. COVER. HOLD ON. Drop to the floor, cover yourself by hiding under a strong piece of furniture, hold on to your cover until the shaking stops.

VERDICT
....
Fake

YOU CAN KEEP HYDRATED BY SUCKING A STONE

FACT OR FAKE?

This is a really old piece of survival advice and it's also pretty silly. The idea is that sucking a stone will trick your mouth into thinking that you are eating and will make your mouth produce saliva, which will keep you hydrated.

TELL ME MORE

The problem with this advice is that you are not actually taking in any new water. Your body produces saliva using water from within the body, so giving your body an extra thing to do is likely to make you even more dehydrated than you were in the first place! There's also the added risk of choking on the stone.

VERDICT
Fake

LOOKING A SHARK IN THE EYE WILL HELP YOU SURVIVE

What are you looking at?

Thankfully, shark attacks are rare. If you do find yourself in the water with a shark, don't panic, it will make the shark more likely to attack. Keep eye contact to show the shark you are not scared. If it comes close, push it gently away – you don't want to make it angry, but you also want to show it that you are tough.

TELL ME MORE

People are not part of a shark's natural diet. Sharks are predators and feed on anything from plankton to fish and seals, depending on the species. In instances of humans being bitten by sharks it is often a case of the shark behaving naturally in its natural habitat. For example, surfers and swimmers have been mistaken for seals.

SHARK STATS

There are 500 species of shark and only around ten species have been involved in attacks on humans. In contrast, a third of shark species are near extinction because of human activity.

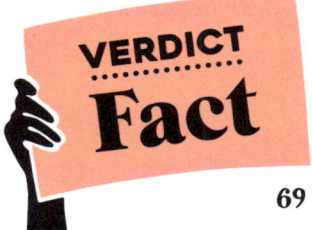

VERDICT
Fact

69

SINKHOLES CAN BE DEEP AND DANGEROUS

Sinkholes are holes that open up in the ground with little or no warning. They can range from small, maybe a metre deep, to vast 50-m-deep pits. There are few signs to show a sinkhole is going to open up. If you see one, call for help straight away and don't go near the edge!

TELL ME MORE

Sinkholes are more common in some parts of the world than others. They happen when rocks or minerals just below the Earth's surface are worn away by water, or when the roof of an underground cave collapses.

SO DEEP!

The biggest sinkhole in the world is in China. The Xiaozhai Tiankeng sinkhole is 626 m long, 537 m wide, and around 600 m deep!

VERDICT
Fact

YOU SHOULD NEVER EAT WEEDS TO SURVIVE

FACT OR FAKE?

While people spend a lot of time growing luscious vegetables, there are lots of tasty and healthy foods growing by themselves – and often getting in the way of the main crop. These are weeds!

TELL ME MORE

Although some will make you ill, lots of weeds can be eaten, so it helps to know about them. In a survival situation they could be vital! Stinging nettles (see page 6) and dandelions are full of nutrition, chickweed and sheep's sorrel can be eaten raw or cooked. Even duckweed, which grows on top of ponds, can be dried to make a nutritious powder.

VERDICT
Fake

BUYING VEG
When compared with some shop-bought leafy greens, some wild weeds have been found to contain higher levels of nutrients!

YOU CAN SURVIVE IN A SUNKEN SHIP

It should be impossible. When a ship sinks, just about every part of it fills with water. Beneath the sea, there is little hope of finding fresh water or food. However, there are two known instances where survival has been possible.

TELL ME MORE

In 2013, a tugboat capsized and sank. One of the crew, Harrison Okene, managed to find an air pocket and was rescued after three days. In 1991, a scuba diver was investigating a wreck when his breathing kit broke. He spent two days in an air pocket eating raw sea urchins before being rescued.

DEEP WATER

When rescued, Harrison Okene had to spend two days in a decompression chamber to recover from spending so long so deep underwater.

VERDICT

Fact

SNAKE BITE KITS ARE ESSENTIAL IN THE WILD

FACT OR FAKE?

If you're heading for a hike in snake country, you might think about taking a snake bite kit with you. But some experts think they are likely to do more harm than good ...

TELL ME MORE

A snake bit kit usually has some kind of suction device that is supposed to pull the venom back out of the bite wound. However, as the venom goes directly into the blood, it moves quickly away from the bite site before you can get the kit out to use it. Working on the wound may also make it worse. Instead, clean the wound and seek medical help!

VERDICT
Fake

KIT BITS

Snake bite kits also include things to treat other insect bites and stings, so those parts of the kits can still be helpful!

A FAMILY PHOTO ▶CAN BE A GOOD◀ SURVIVAL TOOL

FACT OR FAKE?

Of all the things you might hope to have with you when stranded on a desert island, a family photo might not be at the top of your list. But survival experts reckon that this type of reminder of what you have waiting back at home may well be key to survival.

TELL ME MORE

A large part of being able to survive alone in an incredibly difficult situation is in your mindset. Having a photo will help you to maintain the will to succeed at staying alive by giving you a focus and a purpose.

VERDICT
Fact

DON'T PULL YOURSELF OUT OF AN ICE HOLE

While sliding on a frozen river or lake looks fun, it can be dangerous. There may be places where the ice is thin and you can fall through! If you do fall in, get to the solid edge of ice and raise your arms out on top of it. Don't try to pull yourself straight out – it's incredibly difficult.

TELL ME MORE

Instead, try to lift your bottom and kick your legs so that you are horizontal in the water. Kick, pull, kick, pull in this position and try to get out of the hole on your stomach. Once out, don't stand up, you are likely to go through the ice again. Instead, roll or slide away from the hole until you reach the bank.

VERDICT
Fact

COLD SHOCK!
Suddenly going into super cold water will put you in cold shock, making you gasp – try to calm down and steady your breathing.

LIFE COULD SURVIVE ON MARS

Oh hey!

FACT OR FAKE?

Microbes are miniscule life forms or microorganisms. They are so small that you cannot see them without a microscope. They exist in some form in just about every environment on Earth ... but what about in space?

TELL ME MORE

Scientists believe that there was water on the surface of Mars billions of years ago. As water and life usually go together, it is possible that life existed on Mars at that time. The presence of methane in the Martian atmosphere is a possible clue that microorganisms may still be living on Mars. Scientists experiment by recreating the harsh conditions on Mars with microorganisms found on Earth, to see if they can survive.

SPACE STUDIES

Astrobiology is the field of science study that looks at how life forms might exist in space.

VERDICT
almost Fact

MAGGOTS CAN CLEAN WOUNDS

We're here to help

Nom nom, dead tissue

FACT OR FAKE?

This is one of those crazy things you see in films, but it actually works! It is thought that people in ancient times allowed maggots to feed on open or infected wounds, helping them to heal more successfully and the patient to survive.

TELL ME MORE

This maggot munching is so successful that it is now used in modern medicine, too. Maggots are the larvae of flies. They eat any dead tissue, but leave the healthy tissue alone, which allows the wound to heal. Maggots also produce substances that dissolve dead tissue, which they can then take in, along with any bacteria in the wound.

LEECH LOVE

Another handy creature is the leech. Commonly found in wet habitats, the leech can be used in medicine to stimulate blood flow to a damaged limb or digit!

VERDICT
Fact

YOU CAN DRINK WATER FROM A CACTUS

FACT OR FAKE?

If you're stuck in the desert, you might think a cactus will save you. To exist in these dried-out regions, cacti suck up water from the rare rainfalls and store it in their fleshy bodies.

TELL ME MORE

If water from a cactus was easy to get at, they would soon be harvested by every thirsty desert creature and there wouldn't be any left. As well as protecting themselves with sharp spines, most cacti contain chemicals that cause serious illness if eaten or drunk. Two exceptions are the pricky pear cactus (see page 89) and the fishhook barrel cactus.

CACTI LOOKALIKES

Some plants in the family *Euphorbiaceae* look like cacti - they grow in southern Africa and Madagascar. They contain a sticky white sap that is toxic to humans.

VERDICT
....
Fake

Don't worry, I got you

YOU CAN CLEAN WATER WITH SUNLIGHT

FACT OR FAKE?

Imagine you are out in the wilderness. You have a bottle of water, but you're not sure if it's clean enough to drink. What do you do? Leave it in the sunshine, and the sunlight will clean it for you!

TELL ME MORE

Sunlight won't remove any physical dirt from your water, (for that, you'd need to filter it), however, it will remove any germs. Part of sunlight is called ultraviolet, or UV, light. The UV light enters any microorganisms in the water and destroys them.

VERDICT
Fact

BIRDS AND BEES
Humans can't see UV Light, but birds and bees can!

ALWAYS RUN AWAY FROM A LION

FACT OR FAKE?

The fastest human, Usain Bolt, can run at 44 kph, and only for a short distance. Lions can run at 80 kph. You won't be able to outrun a lion, so don't try. Instead, maintain eye contact and back slowly away.

TELL ME MORE

Most lion charges are fake charges, to intimidate you or see what you are going to do. Hold your arms in the air and shout as much as you can. If you have anything, throw it at the lion. If you are in a group, always stick together to make yourselves look as big as possible.

SLEEPY CATS

Lions are usually active for only 4 hours of the day, the rest of the time they sleep!

VERDICT

Fake

DARWIN CAME UP WITH THE PHRASE 'SURVIVAL OF THE FITTEST'

FACT OR FAKE?

In 1859, naturalist Charles Darwin published a book called *On the Origin of Species*. In it he describes how those animals best adapted to their environment will be the ones to survive and reproduce.

VERDICT
Fake

TELL ME MORE

The book became famous, and in a later 1869 edition Darwin used the phrase 'survival of the fittest', and that became famous, too. However, it wasn't Darwin's originally. He borrowed the phrase from philosopher Herbert Spencer, who had used it in his own book in 1864. In another twist, Spencer came up with the phrase after reading Darwin's earlier work.

I thought I'd come up with that ...

ANIMALS CAN

FACT OR FAKE?

Animals can detect smells in two ways: they can pick up the scent molecules of a substance, and they can also pick up chemicals called pheromones given out by other animals, including humans. However, most animals can pick up only the chemical messages of their own species.

VERDICT

PART **Fake**

PART **Fact**

SMELL FEAR

Smells like chicken ... or could be fear ...

TELL ME MORE

Dogs might be a bit different. Researchers have done an experiment to test whether dogs react differently when smelling a T-shirt worn by a frightened person to when smelling a T-shirt worn by a happy person. The dogs that smelled the frightened person's T-shirt showed more stressed behaviour. A similar experiment has also been done with horses!

IN THE NOSE

Dogs have an amazing sense of smell: where humans have around 6 million scent receptors, dogs have as many as 300 million!

TOOTHPASTE CAN HELP TO TREAT INSECT BITES

FACT OR FAKE?

When you are bitten or stung by an insect, the insect injects a chemical into your skin that your body doesn't like. It reacts and causes itching. It's best not to scratch a bite as you can cause further harm by breaking the skin. But what can you do instead?

TELL ME MORE

Adding a dab of toothpaste might seem a bit strange, but it works. The peppermint in the toothpaste adds a cooling sensation, which overtakes the itching signal to your brain. The cooling may also help to reduce swelling.

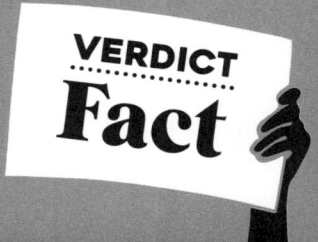

VERDICT
....
Fact

DR NATURE
Other natural bite remedies include honey, basil, vinegar and teabags!

YOU CAN COLLECT WATER FROM A TREE

FACT OR FAKE?

Collecting water from a tree makes use of a tree's natural system of transpiration. Trees take in water from the ground, use it to make food and then release some of the water through little holes in their leaves.

TELL ME MORE

If you tie a plastic bag carefully around a leafy branch, trapping the leaves inside, the water released by the leaves will collect in the bag. It will condense against the plastic and run to the bottom of the bag. As long as the leaves and bag are clean, you can then drink the water!

I'm so awesome

VERDICT
Fact

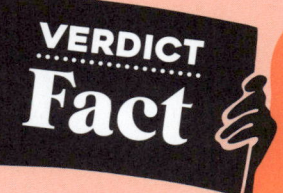

TASTING TREES

Different trees make different tasting water! However, poisonous plants or trees may also make water containing toxins, so be careful which tree you choose.

INSIDE A SNOW HOLE IS EVEN COLDER THAN OUTSIDE

FACT OR FAKE?

Building a snow hole is a great way to make an emergency shelter – but it might take a little while! You need to find a bank of snow that is quite solid and not wet, and, if possible, in a sheltered place out of the wind.

TELL ME MORE

Dig straight back into the snow and upwards until you can sit up comfortably. Then dig sleeping bunks into the walls – having these off the floor will allow cold air to sink below you, keeping you snug. A snow hole can have temperatures of 0°C or more, even when the air outside is much lower!

SNOW TOOLS

It's useful to carry a snow shovel and even a snow saw when you are adventuring in the snow!

VERDICT

Fake

YOU CAN COLLECT DEW IF YOU ARE THIRSTY

FACT OR FAKE?

Dew is the light misty water vapour that settles on the ground in the early morning. In the driest regions of the world, people have made use of this reliable water source for thousands of years.

TELL ME MORE

Archaeologists have found evidence of ancient peoples in South America and Egypt building stone piles to collect dew. If you're stuck, hang clean clothing out at night and wring the dew from it in the early morning to drink. You can also run a clean cloth through plants and leaves to collect the dew sitting on them.

DEW NEED HELP?

Dew and early morning fog are harvested to help people who have little or no access to clean water.

VERDICT

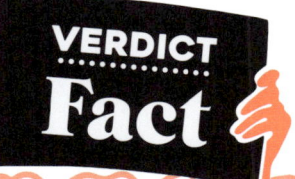

Fact

PLAY DEAD IF YOU ARE ATTACKED BY A BEAR

FACT OR FAKE?

If you find yourself face to face with a bear, there are a lot of don'ts to remember: don't run away, don't climb a tree, don't play dead – unless you are faced with a grizzly bear!

TELL ME MORE

Don't try to scare a bear or frighten it away, you are likely to make it attack. You should walk backwards slowly, with your arms in the air and talk in a calm voice. If the bear attacks, fight back with anything you can find – fists, rocks, branches. But, if it's a grizzly bear, play dead: roll onto your stomach, cover your head with your arms and keep your backpack on!

BEAR ID

Brown and grizzly bears are the same species – brown bears are coastal, grizzlies live inland. Black bears are smaller and blacker in colour.

VERDICT

PART Fake

PART Fact

YOU CAN'T EAT SPIKY PLANTS

FACT OR FAKE?

Foraging means looking for food in the wild. Don't eat spiky plants is one of the pieces of advice given, but what about thistles and prickly pear cacti? You can eat both of those!

TELL ME MORE

The problem with thistles is the spikes – you need to wear gloves if you are going to pick them. Once stripped of spikes, you can eat the stalk. Pricky pears are the fruit of a cactus – you can eat the fruit and the leaf pads once the spines are removed. There are many foods in the wild that you can eat and many others that make you ill. Don't pick anything unless you know exactly what it is!

FUNNY FAMILIES

The super-poisonous plant hemlock is in the same plant family as carrots, parsley and fennel.

VERDICT
Fake

89

A MAN LIVED FOR TWO MONTHS IN HIS CAR, UNDER THE SNOW

FACT OR FAKE?

When snowmobile riders uncovered a car buried in snow on a deserted road in Sweden in 2012, they had no idea what they would find inside. There was a man, curled in a sleeping bag, with only comic books for company and snow for food. He had been there for two months.

TELL ME MORE

Doctors think that the man was able to stay alive because the snow that covered his car created an igloo effect – insulating the vehicle so that the temperature never reached the -22°C that it was outside. Another doctor said he may have gone into a near-hibernation state where his body required very little energy.

ICE-INSULATION

Snow is made of ice and air. The air that is trapped between the snow crystals helps to stop warmth passing through and escaping.

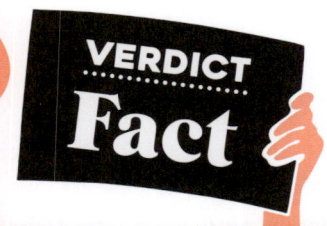

VERDICT
Fact

YOU CAN MAKE FIRE FROM ICE

But I'll melt!

First you need a clear block of ice. Then you need to chip away until you have a round disk shape – like a circle with domed surfaces.

TELL ME MORE

The next step is to shape and polish it so that it is smooth. You can use a rock to rub it smooth and then polish it with the warmth of your hands. When you hold your ice lens between the Sun and the ground you should see a bright light spot appear. Angle this on to some dry tinder and it will concentrate the Sun's heat enough in one spot to set the tinder alight!

VERDICT

Fact

GLOSSARY

amputate – to cut off part of the body

analogue – a watch that shows the time with hands as pointers, rather than an electronic display showing numbers

anchor – to hold yourself firmly in one place

Andes – a range of mountains in South America

bacteria – a microorganism that can cause disease

condo – short for condominium, a block apartments

conserve – to protect something from loss, waste or harm

crevasse – a deep, open crack, such as in a glacier

debris – pieces of rubbish that are scattered about

decompression chamber – a small room in which you can adjust the air pressure. It is used by deep-sea divers when they need to readjust to surface level, or normal, air pressure.

dehydrate – when the body loses a large amount of water

disorientated – when you have lost your sense of direction

distress – a state of great need or trouble

ember – a small piece of hot glowing wood

environment – the surroundings in which a person or animal lives

expedition – a journey planned and taken by people for a specific purpose

fibres – threads of material that come from a plant

filtration – the process of putting a liquid through a filter to clean it

friction – one surface rubbing against another

frostbite – an injury where body tissue is damaged by being exposed to extreme cold

germs – microorganisms that cause illness and disease

hibernation – a state of deep sleep that an animal or plant goes into during winter

horizontal – in line with the horizon, lying flat rather than upright or vertical

hypothermia – a condition where the body temperature falls dangerously low, causing difficulty in performing normal actions

ice floe – a sheet of floating ice

infection – illness caused by germs getting into the body

insulate – to protect something by wrapping it in a material that prevents it losing heat

intimidate – to frighten something or someone

landmark – an object or formation in the landscape that can be easily recognised

medicinally – to be used for medical reasons

methane – a colourless, odourless gas

microorganism – a tiny organism, especially a bacterium or virus

Morse code – an alphabet of symbols, where each letter is represented by a different series of dots and dashes

navigation – the process of finding out your position and planning a route to a destination

northern hemisphere – the half of Earth that is above the equator (an invisible line that runs around Earth at an equal distance from the poles)

nutrients – substances that the body needs to grow and live

nutritious – rich in nutrients, (see previous entry)

parasite – an organism that exists on or in a host organism, using the host's resources to survive

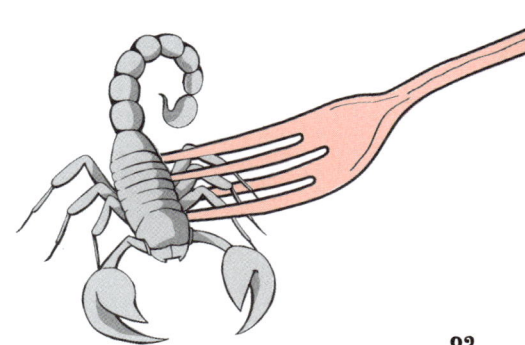

pathogen – a type of disease-causing microorganism

poisonous – a substance causing illness or death if taken into the body

provisions – supplies of food, drink and equipment for a journey

radiation – a type of energy released by some objects that can cause damage to organisms

saliva – a liquid produced in the mouth to help with digestion

silo – a tall underground chamber used for storage or to keep a missile ready to fire

southern hemisphere – the half of Earth that is below the equator (an invisible line that runs around Earth at an equal distance from the poles)

symmetrical – having the same appearance on each side of a central line

tectonic plates – the sections of Earth's crust and mantle that move very slowly, they are the cause of earthquakes and volcanic eruptions

transpiration – the action of a plant letting water vapour out of tiny holes (stomata) in its leaves

trawler – a boat used for trawler fishing, where a net is pulled through the water

venom – a poisonous substance carried by some animals, such as snakes and scorpions

vital – necessary or essential

FURTHER INFORMATION

BOOKS

How to Survive in the Ocean/ Desert/Mountain (Tough Guides)
by Louise Spilsbury, (Wayland, 2018)

Science for Surviving in Space (Space Science)
by Mark Thompson, (Wayland, 2020)

Science Adventures series
by Richard and Louise Spilsbury, (Franklin Watts, 2017)

Shackleton's Journey
by William Gill, (Flying Eye Books, 2014)

Survival for Beginners: A Step-by-Step Guide to Camping and Outdoor Skills
by Colin Towell, (DK Children, 2019)

WEBSITES

www.scouts.org.uk/scouts/awards/
Have a look through the Scout organisation award pages for information on their survival skills award.

www.rgs.org/schools/teaching-resources/subject-knowledge-animation-shackleton/
Learn more about Ernest Shackleton's famous expedition with the Royal Geographic Society website.

seahistory.org/sea-history-for-kids/navigating-by-the-stars/
Find out more about navigating by the stars with this page from the National Maritime Historical Society.

INDEX